Please visit our website, www.enslow.com.
For a free color catalog of all our high-quality books, call toll free
1-800-398-2504 or fax 1-877-980-4454.

Cataloging-in-Publication Data

Names: Emminizer, Theresa.
Title: Who puts out wildfires? / Theresa Emminizer.
Description: Buffalo, NY : Enslow Publishing, 2025. | Series: Calling all community heroes! | Includes glossary and index.
Identifiers: ISBN 9781978542211 (pbk.) | ISBN 9781978542228 (library bound) | ISBN 9781978542235 (ebook)
Subjects: LCSH: Wildfires–Juvenile literature. | Wildfire fighters–Juvenile literature.
| First responders–Juvenile literature.
Classification: LCC SD421.23 E495 2025 | DDC 363.37'9–dc23

Published in 2025 by
Enslow Publishing
2544 Clinton Street
Buffalo, NY 14224

Copyright © 2025 Enslow Publishing

Designer: Tanya Dellaccio Keeney
Editor: Theresa Emminizer

Photo credits: Cover (background) ASTA DESIGN/Shutterstock.com; cover (speech bubble) mejorana/Shutterstock.com; cover (firefighter) Kzenon/Shutterstock.com; cover (wildfire) Alaskagirl8821/Shutterstock.com; p.5 Christian Roberts-Olsen/Shutterstock.com; pp. 7, 17 Gorodenkoff/Shutterstock.com; p. 9 Richard Thornton/Shutterstock.com; p. 11 Thommy TFH/Shutterstock.com; p. 13 Toa55/Shutterstock.com; p 15 Kaweepol_Kan/Shutterstock.com; p. 19 Christine Bird/Shutterstock.com; p. 21 DNB STOCK/Shutterstock.com.

All rights reserved.
No part of this book may be reproduced in any form without permission in writing from the publisher, except by a reviewer.

Printed in the United States of America

Some of the images in this book illustrate individuals who are models. The depictions do not imply actual situations or events.

CPSIA compliance information: Batch #CWENS25: For further information contact Enslow Publishing, at 1-800-398-2504.

CONTENTS

WHAT'S A WILDFIRE?...........4
WHO'S CALLED TO WILDFIRES?...6
FIREFIGHTING CREWS..........8
ENGINE, FUEL, AND
HAND CREWS.................10
HELITACK CREWS
AND SMOKEJUMPERS..........12
INTERAGENCY HOTSHOT CREWS..14
HOTSHOT TRAINING...........16
FIREFIGHTING TOOLS.........18
PRACTICE FIRE SAFETY.......20
WORDS TO KNOW.............22
FOR MORE INFORMATION......23
INDEX.....................24

BOLDFACE WORDS APPEAR IN WORDS TO KNOW.

WHAT'S A WILDFIRE?

Wildfires are large, deadly fires that burn in natural areas, such as forests. Wildfires can happen anytime, anywhere. They spread quickly and cause great harm, burning plants, trees, and homes as they go. The smoke from wildfires is deadly too.

 DUE TO CLIMATE CHANGE, WILDFIRES HAVE BEEN GETTING STRONGER AND HAPPENING MORE OFTEN.

WHO'S CALLED TO WILDFIRES?

When a wildfire happens in a national forest, the U.S. Forest Service leads the **response**. Forest Service firefighters may work closely with firefighters from other local or government **agencies** such as the National Interagency Fire Center (NIFC).

 THERE ARE MORE THAN 10,000 FIREFIGHTERS IN THE U.S. FOREST SERVICE.

FIREFIGHTING CREWS

All firefighters must go through special training and learn how to use different kinds of tools. There are different kinds of firefighting crews:

- engine
- hand
- smokejumpers
- interagency hotshot crews.
- fuel
- helitack

Each crew has its own set of skills.

 IN THIS PICTURE, FIREFIGHTERS ARE LEARNING HOW TO DO A HELICOPTER RESCUE.

ENGINE, FUEL, AND HAND CREWS

Engine crews lead the first attack on wildfires. They use equipment, or tools, from the fire engine, such as heavy hoses. Fuel crews clear away anything that might fuel, or power, the fire, such as wood or dry plants. Hand crews build fire lines.

FIREBREAK

 A FIRE LINE OR FIREBREAK IS AN AREA OF CLEARED LAND MADE TO STOP A FIRE FROM SPREADING.

HELITACK CREWS AND SMOKEJUMPERS

Helitack crews fly helicopters into fires. They drop water and **fire retardant** onto the fire from above. They also bring tools and more firefighters to ground crews and help build fire lines. Smokejumpers **parachute** from airplanes to bring help to ground crews as fast as possible.

 THIS HELICOPTER IS CARRYING A WATER BUCKET TO DUMP ONTO A FIRE.

INTERAGENCY HOTSHOT CREWS

A hotshot is a firefighter who works on the front lines. They go directly into the hottest, most dangerous, or unsafe, parts of the fire. Hotshot crews are made up of highly skilled, highly trained firefighters with lots of **experience**. Many also have **medical** training.

 HOTSHOTS ARE THE SPECIAL FORCES OF FIREFIGHTING.

HOTSHOT TRAINING

In addition to their skilled training, hotshots must also pass certain tests. They need to be able to run 1.5 miles (2.4 km) in 10 minutes and 35 seconds or less. They must also do 40 sit-ups in 60 seconds and 25 push-ups in 60 seconds.

 HOTSHOTS MUST BE VERY STRONG.

FIREFIGHTING TOOLS

Firefighters use fire engines, helicopters, planes, and large aircraft called airtankers to fight wildfires. They wear **protective** clothing such as helmets, eyewear, gloves, and boots to keep themselves safe. Axes, chain saws, shovels, and blades are important hand tools.

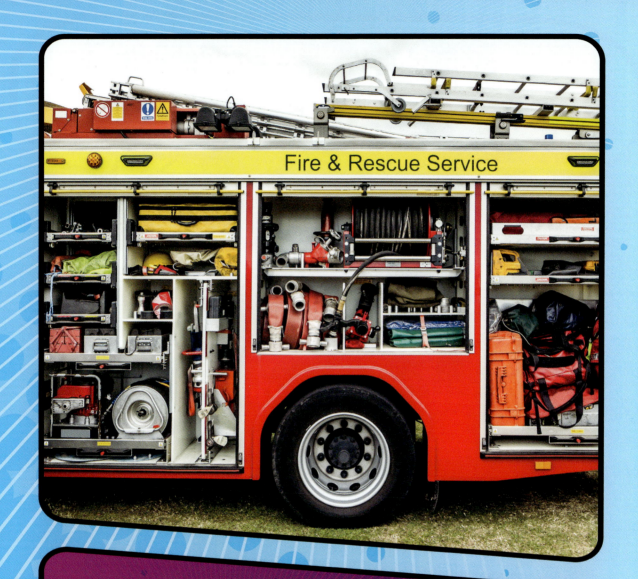

 FIRE ENGINES ARE FILLED WITH USEFUL TOOLS.

PRACTICE FIRE SAFETY

There are more than 73,000 wildfires in the United States each year. Thankfully, firefighters are here to help! You can help **prevent** wildfires by practicing fire safety. Never play with fire or go near a fire without a grown-up nearby. Call 911 if an unplanned fire starts.

 MANY PARKS HAVE SIGNS LIKE THIS ONE THAT SAY IF WILDFIRE RISK IS HIGH.

WORDS TO KNOW

agency: A division of a government that provides a particular service.

climate change: Long-term change in Earth's climate, most recently global warming caused by human activities such as burning oil and natural gas.

experience: Skills gained by doing something many times.

fire retardant: Substances that often slow or stop the spread of fire.

medical: Having to do with care given by doctors.

parachute: To drop from an aircraft using a device made of cloth that slows the fall.

prevent: To stop something from happening.

protective: Made to keep something or someone safe.

response: A reaction to something that has happened.

risk: The chance that something bad will happen.

FOR MORE INFORMATION

BOOKS

Murray, Laura K. *Firefighters*. Mankato, MN: Creative Education and Creative Paperbacks, 2023.

Jaycox, Jaclyn. *Wildfire: Inside the Inferno*. North Mankato, MN: Capstone editions, an imprint of Capstone, 2023.

WEBSITES

Ready Kids
www.ready.gov/kids/disaster-facts/wildfires
Find out how you can stay safe and prepare for wildfires.

Smokey Bear
www.smokeybear.com/en/smokey-for-kids/preventing-wildfires
Learn Smokey's five tips for preventing forest fires.

Publisher's note to educators and parents: Our editors have carefully reviewed these websites to ensure that they are suitable for students. Many websites change frequently, however, and we cannot guarantee that a site's future contents will continue to meet our high standards of quality and educational value. Be advised that students should be closely supervised whenever they access the internet.

INDEX

airtankers, 18
clothing, 18
fire engine, 10, 18, 19
fire lines, 10, 11, 12
hand tools, 18
helicopters, 9, 12, 13
hotshots, 14, 15, 16, 17
national forest, 6
National Interagency Fire Center (NIFC), 6

911, 20
parks, 21
physical tests, 16
signs, 21
skills, 8
smoke, 4
U.S. Forest Service, 6, 7
water, 12, 13